Terry—

Happy Birthday

my very dear friend

Love,
Gloria
7/16/02

Blessings of Friendship

Always There for Me

By Flavia and Lisa Weedn
Illustrated by Flavia Weedn

Cedco Publishing · San Rafael, California

ISBN 0-7683-2152-2

Text by Flavia and Lisa Weedn
Illustrations by Flavia Weedn
© Weedn Family Trust
www.flavia.com
All rights reserved.

Published in 2000 by Cedco Publishing Company.
100 Pelican Way, San Rafael, California 94901
For a free catalog of other Cedco® products, please write to the
address above, or visit our website: www.cedco.com

Printed in Hong Kong

1 3 5 7 9 10 8 6 4 2

Book and jacket layout by Teena Gores

The artwork for each picture is
digitally mastered using acrylic on canvas.

Because

you're my

friend,

we've

shared

dreams

and

tears . . .

laughter and disappointments.

You know the things I

dream of

and

the things

I'll never

be.

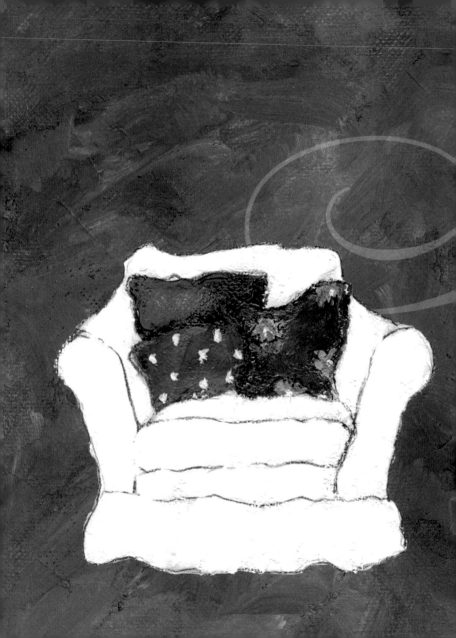

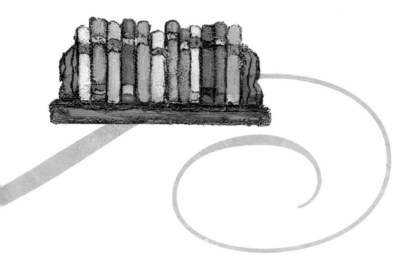

You're

always

there

when I
need
you.

You

listen

and you

understand.

I'll always be

here

for you,

and

I'll

catch

you

if

you

should

ever

fall.

I'll
care
how you feel
when you lose

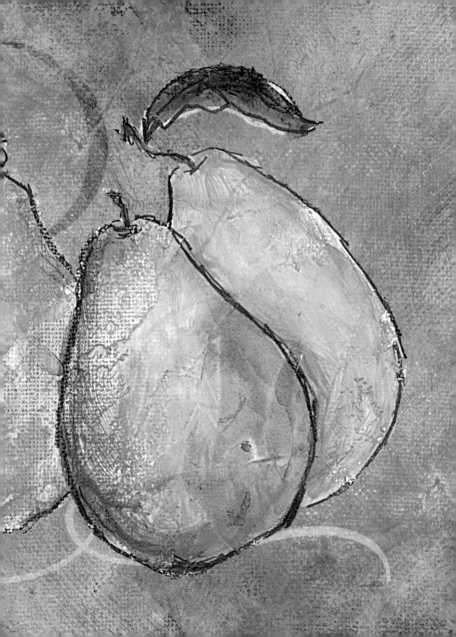

and be

with you

when you're afraid.

You'll

always be

a part of my

life...